OUR UNITED STATES GEOGRAPHY: OUR REGIONS AND PEOPLE WORKBOOK

by
Beverly Vaillancourt

The Peoples Publishing Group, Inc.

Free to Learn, to Grow, to Change

ISBN1-56256-120-0

© 1994
The Peoples Publishing Group, Inc.
299 Market Street
Saddle Brook NJ 07663

Printed in the United States of America
16   17   18   19

Credits

Editing by *Jocelyn Chu*
Editorial Assistance by Daniel Ortiz, Jr.
Copyediting by Sal Allocco
Editorial & Electronic Design Assistance by Sharen J. Levine and Jocelyn Chu
Map Design by Steve Steiner, Cartographer
Electronic Publishing Consultant: James Fee Langendoen
Cover Design by Klaus Spitzenberger, Westchester Graphics Group
Logo Design by Wendy E. Kury
Reader Reviews by Leslie Fishbein and Faith Allen, special education and multicultural educators, and Neil Steiner, middle school geography teacher

A special thanks to the many educators and administrators around the country who participated in a research survey related to the revision of this text.

GETTING READY...

The activities in this workbook will help you to remember facts about each state. You will be asked to answer review questions. The answer to each question can be found in your textbook.

More detailed GeoFacts are given for each state. At times you will use these GeoFacts to set up a graph. Watch for these new GeoFacts!

For each chapter, you will be asked to add some information to the state. Often you will be asked to color and label certain parts of the map. You will need to check other books such as encyclopedias or almanacs for the information you need. In this way, not only will your map-reading skills improve, but you also will have the chance to use reference books. You will need colored pencils, a ruler, and a pencil to complete the activities in this book.

TABLE OF CONTENTS

OUR UNITED STATES ★ ★ ★ ★ ★ ★ ★

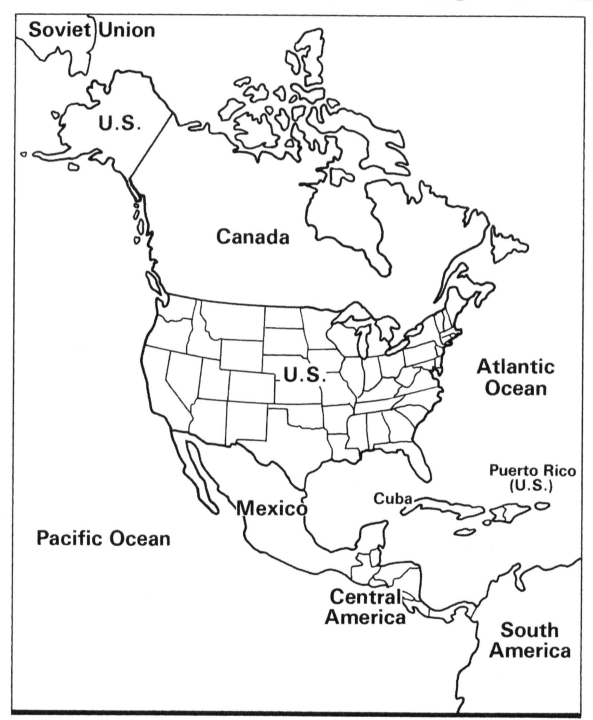

OUR UNITED STATES — THE LAND

Read the **Passport to Discovery!** section in your textbook. Then do the following:

1. Color the water area all around the continent of North America blue.

2. Label the Atlantic Ocean.

3. Label the Pacific Ocean.

4. Color the five Great Lakes blue.

5. Color the country of Canada orange.

6. Color the country of Mexico red.

7. Label Alaska.

 Our United States Geography Workbook

OUR UNITED STATES — THE PEOPLE

The following numbers tell how many people lived in the United States for nine different years that people were counted. Use dots to plot the numbers on the graph. Then draw a line connecting the dots.

1900 — 76,212,168	1930 — 123,202,624	1960 — 179,323,175
1910 — 92,228,496	1940 — 132,164,569	1970 — 203,302,031
1920 — 106,021,537	1950 — 151,325,798	1980 — 226,542,203

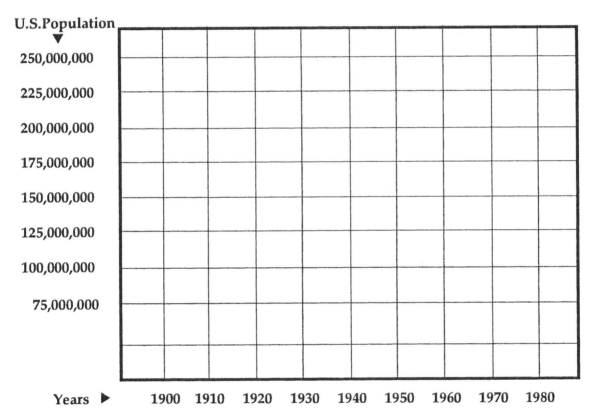

1. Between which years was there the greatest increase in the number of people living in the United States? _____

2. Between which years was there the slowest growth in the number of people living in the United States? _____

3. How many people do you think will be living in the United States in the year 2,000? _____

Across the South ★ ★ ★ ★ ★ ★ ★ ★ ★ ★ ★ ★

Map Study

1. Color the Gulf of Mexico and the Atlantic Ocean blue.

2. Color the states which have borders along the Gulf of Mexico green.

3. Color the states which have borders along the Atlantic Ocean yellow.

4. Color the Across the South state that is farthest north orange.

5. Color the Across the South state that is farthest south brown.

6. Which state was colored the most colors?_____

7. Which state was not colored? _____

8. Which state shares borders with both the Gulf of Mexico and the Atlantic Ocean?

_____

        Our United States Geography Workbook

GeoThoughts

Think about what it must have been like to be escaping from slavery along the Underground Railroad. Put yourself in the place of an enslaved African escaping from the cruel life of slavery. Write a paragraph about one of the days in your journey to freedom.

_____

_____

_____

_____

_____

_____

_____

_____

_____

_____

 ## Spotlight

Cashimir Pulaski was born in Poland in 1747. He met Benjamin Franklin in France in the 1770s. Learning of America's fight for freedom, Pulaski traveled to America. Once he arrived in America, Pulaski joined George Washington's forces. He was a hero in battle, so Congress awarded him the rank of general. Soon Pulaski led his force against the British army. He died two days after being wounded in a battle over Savannah, Georgia. By act of Congress, October 11 is honored as Pulaski Day.

ARKANSAS ★ ★ ★ ★ ★ ★ ★ ★ ★ ★ ★ ★ ★ ★ ★ ★ ★ ★

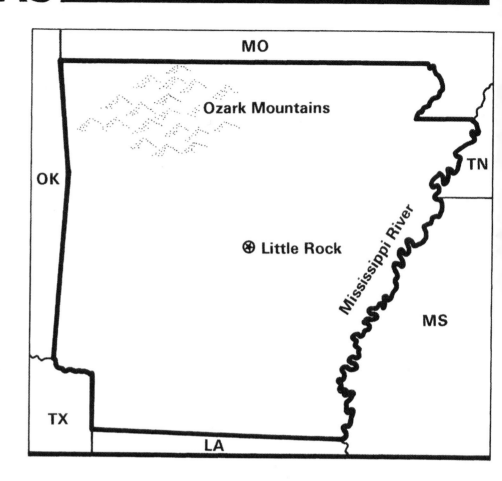

GEOFACTS
total area: 53,187 square miles
inland water: 1,109 square miles
population: 2,350,725
largest city: Little Rock

GEOWORDS
folktales
enslave
mounds
readmit

Know Arkansas

1. What explorer from Spain came to Arkansas in 1544? _____

2. What area lies along the Arkansas River? _____

3. What are "hot springs"? _____

4. What three products add to the economy of Alabama? _____

   _____.

Map Study

1. Use blue to draw the Arkansas River. Label the river.
2. Think of a map key symbol for the Quachita Mountains. Use green to add the Quachita Mountains to the map.
3. Use brown to fill in the Arkansas River Valley.
4. Use blue to draw the Spring River. Label the river.
5. Trace the Mississippi River in blue.

    Our United States Geography Workbook

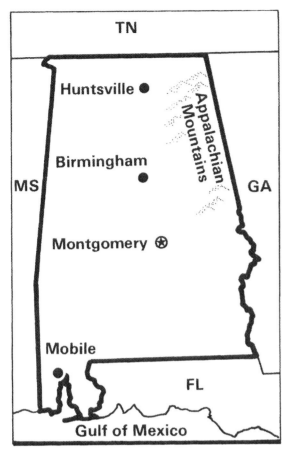

GEOFACTS
total area: 51,705 square miles
inland water: 938 square miles
population: 4,040,587
largest city: Birmingham

GEOWORDS
landlocked
harbor
fertile

Know Alabama

1. _____ have always been important to Alabama's economy.

2. At one time, people had to pay _____ before they could vote.

3. Five crops that grow well in Alabama are _____

_____.

4. There is an important waterway for Alabama that cuts the number of miles boats need to travel to get

to the Gulf of Mexico. This waterway is called _____.

Map Study

1. Use orange to fill in the area called the Mobile River Delta.
2. Use blue to color the Gulf of Mexico.
3. Use blue to draw the Tennessee River.
4. Use blue to draw the Tombighee River.
5. Color Alabama's Black Belt region yellow.

MISSISSIPPI ★ ★ ★ ★ ★ ★ ★ ★ ★ ★ ★ ★ ★ ★ ★ ★ ★ ★

GEOFACTS
total area: 47,689 square miles
inland water: 456 square miles
population: 2,573,216
largest city: Jackson

GEOWORDS
trawl
dike
hurricane

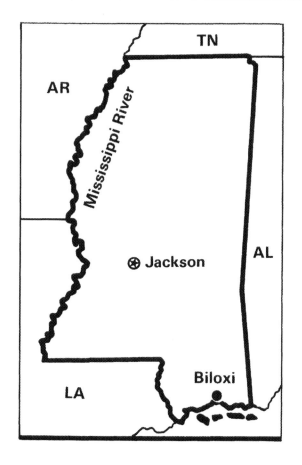

Know Mississippi

1. _____ built along the Mississippi River help to control flooding.

2. One crop that has affected much of Mississippi's past is _____.

3. The sale of _____ , _____ , and _____ are important to Mississippi's economy.

4. Two other industries important to Mississippi's economy are _____ and _____ .

Map Study

1. Trace the Mississippi River and color the Gulf of Mexico in blue.
2. Draw the Big Black River and the Pearl River in blue.
3. Add dots on the map to show where the cities of Gulfport, Tupelo, and Vicksburg are. Label the cities.
4. Color Mississippi's Black Belt region yellow.
5. Color Mississippi's coastal area red.

 Our United States Geography Workbook

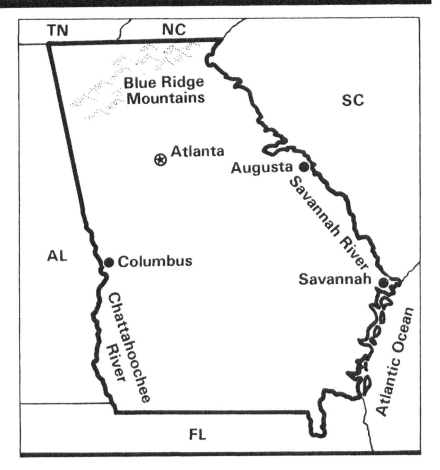

GEOFACTS
  total area: 58,910 square miles
  inland water: 854 square miles
  population: 6,478,216
  largest city: Atlanta

GEOWORDS
  plain

Know Georgia

1. Two crops that grow well in Georgia are _____ .

2. Georgia is also called the _____ State.

3. Which land region covers about one-third of the state? _____

4. Two other land regions in Georgia are the _____ and

   the _____ .

Map Study

1. Color Georgia's piedmont region yellow.
2. Draw the Chattahoochee River and the Savannah River in blue.
3. Use your mountain map symbol. Add the Cohutta Mountains to the map. Label the mountains.
4. Color the Atlantic Ocean blue.
5. Use dots to add in the cities of Albany, Brunswick, and Athens. Label the cities.

LOUISIANA ★★★★★★★★★★★★★★★★

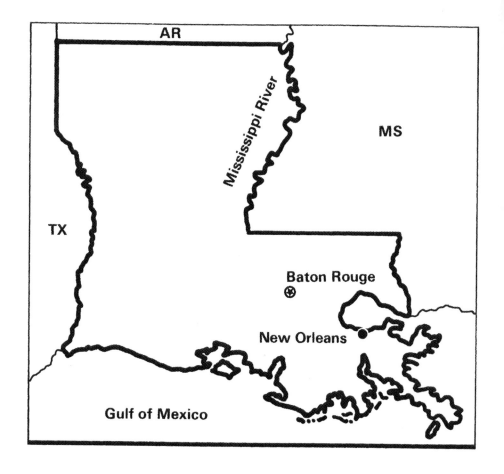

GEOFACTS
total area: 47,751 square miles
inland water: 3,230 square miles
population: 4,219,973
largest city: New Orleans

GEOWORDS
delta
meandering
banks
bayou
humid
brackish
levee

Know Louisiana

1. Which land region in Louisiana grows in size each year? _____

2. Louisiana's first settlers were Native American _____.

3. _____ built along river banks help to hold back flooding.

4. _____ water is water that is very salty.

Map Study

1. Using blue, first trace and then finish drawing the Mississippi River.
2. Using dots, add in the cities of Alexandria, Shreveport, Lake Charles, and New Iberia. Label the cities.
3. Draw the Red River in blue.
4. Color Louisiana's Delta region green.
5. Color the Gulf of Mexico blue.

 Our United States Geography Workbook

★ ★ ★ ★ ★ ★ ★ ★ SOUTH CAROLINA

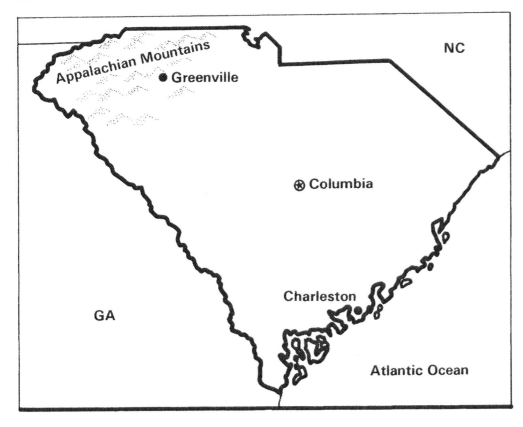

GEOFACTS
total area: 31,113 square miles
inland water: 910 square miles
population: 3,386,703
largest city: Columbia

GEOWORDS
channels
inland
bay

Know South Carolina

1. South Carolina is divided into two areas: the _____ and

   the _____ .

2. _____ covers South Carolina's upland area.

3. The edge of South Carolina's piedmont is marked by the _____

   _____

4. South Carolina's leading crops are _____ , _____ ,

   and _____ .

Map Study

1. Color South Carolina's coastal plain green.
2. Color South Carolina's piedmont region orange.
3. Color South Carolina's mountain region brown.
4. Draw the Broad River, Congaree River, and Santee River in blue. Label each river.
5. Add Lake Marion to the map. Color the lake and the Atlantic Ocean blue.

NORTH CAROLINA ★ ★ ★ ★ ★ ★ ★

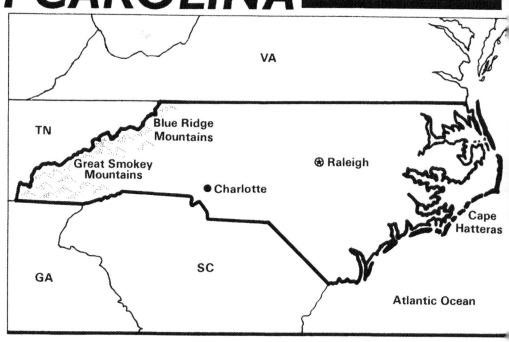

GEOFACTS
total area: 52,669 square miles
inland water: 3,826 square miles
population: 6,628,637
largest city: Charlotte

GEOWORDS
sand dunes
shoreline
sandbars
peak
tornado

Know North Carolina

1. North Carolina has over _____ miles of shoreline.

2. Sandy areas called _____ rise above shallow waters along North Carolina's shoreline.

3. Rising above North Carolina's piedmont region are the _____ .

4. _____ factories and _____ are two important industries in North Carolina.

Map Study

1. Color North Carolina's coastal plain green.
2. Color North Carolina's piedmont area orange.
3. Color North Carolina's mountain area brown.
4. Color the Atlantic Ocean blue.
5. Think of a map key symbol for mountain peaks. Add Mount Mitchell to the map. Label the mountain.

 Our United States Geography Workbook

GEOFACTS
total area: 58,644 square miles
inland water: 4,511 square miles
population: 12,937,926
largest city: Jacksonville

GEOWORDS
endangered
sinkholes

Know Florida

1. Underground water cutting through limestone can cause _____ to form.

2. Florida's _____ has rolling hills and valleys.

3. The sale of such _____ as oranges and grapefruits are important to the economy of Florida.

4. Nine cities in Florida are among the _____ growing cities in the United States.

Map Study

1. Color Lake Okeechobee, the Gulf of Mexico, and the Atlantic Ocean blue.
2. Color the Everglades green.
3. Draw the Suwannee River in blue. Label the river.
4. Label the Florida Keys.
5. Use dots to add in the cities of Ft. Lauderdale, Orlando, and St. Petersburg. Label the cities.

The Appalachian Chain

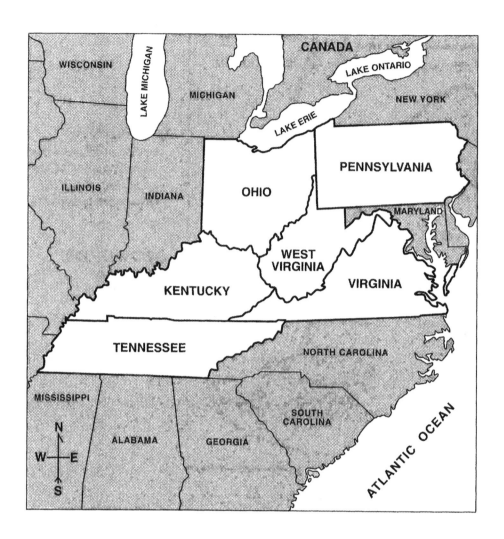

Map Study

1. Color the Great Lakes and Atlantic Ocean blue.

2. Color Canada red.

3. Use a mountain symbol to show the line of the Appalachian Mountains. Your mountain symbol should begin in New York and travel several states to the southwest.

4. Using blue, add the Ohio River to the map. Label the river.

5. Using blue, show where the Mississippi River borders two Appalachian Chain states.

 Our United States Geography Workbook

GeoThoughts

A huge crack in the earth's crust is called a "fault."

Earthquakes happen when there is movement along a fault. Sometimes one area of land will rise above an joining piece of land along a fault line. Sometimes one piece of land will fall below a joining piece of land along a fault line. Another type of movement happens when one piece of land slides sideways along a joining piece of land. Such movements along fault lines can cause either mild or very strong earthquakes. This depends on the amount of movement.

Look up earthquakes in the encyclopedia. Then draw the three types of movements along fault lines.

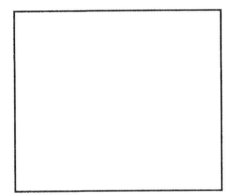 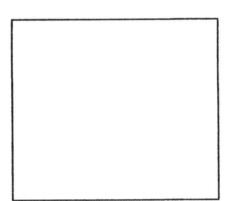 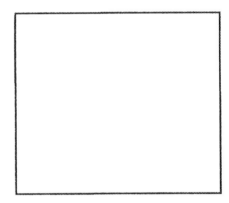

1. UPWARD MOVEMENT   **2. DOWNWARD MOVEMENT**   **3. SIDEWAYS MOVEMENT**

 Spotlight

Rita Dove was born in Akron, Ohio in 1953. In 1970, she was named a presidential scholar. She graduated from Miami University in Oxford, Ohio, with high honors. In 1987, she won the Pulitzer Prize for poetry for "Thomas and Beulah." In 1993, Rita Dove was named the nation's poet laureate by the Library of Congress. Rita Dove is the first African American woman to receive this high national honor.

PENNSYLVANIA ★ ★ ★ ★ ★ ★ ★ ★ ★ ★ ★ ★

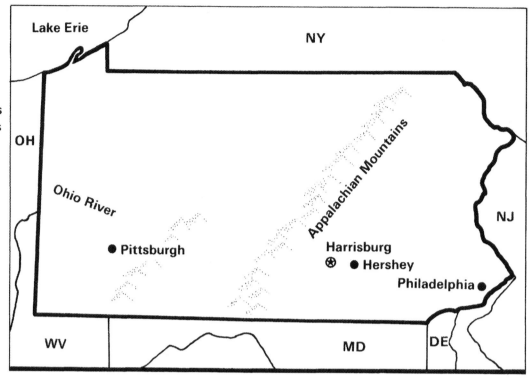

GEOFACTS

total area: 45,308 square miles
inland water: 420 square miles
population: 11,881,643
largest city: Philadelphia

GEOWORDS

resource
fossil
scenic
bed

Know Pennsylvania

1. The Appalachian Mountains were formed by a ———————————— of the earth's crust.

2. ———————————— built across rivers help to control flooding.

3. Three crops important to Pennsylvania's economy are ————————————————————

———————————————— .

4. The Erie Lowland region was once the ———————————— of a lake.

Map Study

1. Draw the Susquehanna River in blue. Color Lake Erie in blue.
2. Label the Allegheny Mountains. Then color the area covered by the Allegheny Mountains and Appalachian Mountains brown.
3. Color the Erie Lowland yellow.
4. Think of map symbols for potatoes, corn, mushrooms, and coal. Add your symbols to the correct place on the map.
5. Add symbols for two other crops or industries important to Pennsylvania's economy.

 Our United States Geography Workbook

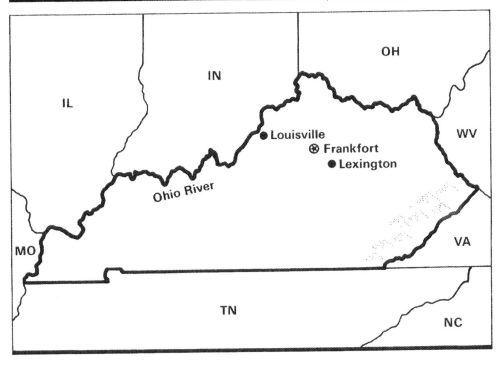

GEOFACTS
total area: 40, 409 square miles
inland water: 740 square miles
population: 3,685,296
largest city: Louisville

GEOWORDS
wilderness
tract
pasture
environment

Know Kentucky

1. Millions of years ago, a large _____ covered present-day Kentucky.

2. Kentucky's bluegrass region was once covered by _____ .

3. Today, most coal is mined by _____ the land.

4. Bluegrass grows well in soils rich in _____ .

Map Study

1. Trace the Ohio River in blue.

2. Think of a map symbol for a national park. Now use your symbol to locate Mammoth Cave National Park on the map.

3. Label the Appalachian Mountains. Color the mountain area brown.

4. Think of map symbols for three crops and two natural resources important to Kentucky's economy. Add the symbols to the correct place on the map.

5. Make a map key for the map.

WEST VIRGINIA ★ ★ ★ ★ ★ ★ ★ ★ ★ ★ ★ ★ ★

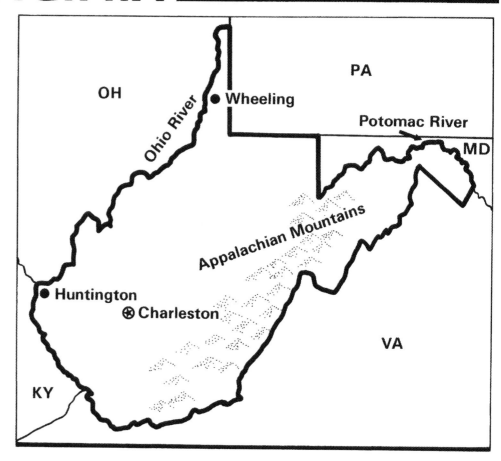

GEOFACTS

total area: 24,231 square miles
inland water: 112 square miles
population: 1,793,477
largest city: Charleston

GEOWORDS

horizon
erosion
panhandle
upland
slope

Know West Virginia

1. Three kinds of trees found in West Virginia are _____ ,

   and _____ .

2. Which mountains in West Virginia rise more than 4,000 feet above sea level? _____

   _____

3. _____ rock forms much of the Blue Ridge Mountains.

4. The mountains of West Virginia are rich in _____ .

Map Study

1. Trace the Potomac River and the Ohio River in blue.

2. Use blue to add Tygart Lake, Sutton Lake, and Summersville Lake to the map.

3. Color the Allegheny Mountains brown, the Blue Ridge Mountains orange, and the Appalachian Plateau yellow.

4. Use a resource map to find out where coal is mined in West Virginia. Add your coal map symbol to the correct places on the map.

5. Add map symbols for three crops grown in West Virginia.

 Our United States Geography Workbook

VIRGINIA

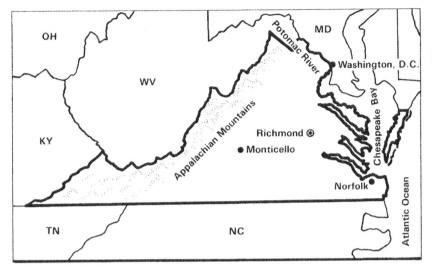

GEOFACTS
total area: 40,767 square miles
inland water: 1,063 square miles
population: 6,187,358
largest city: Virginia Beach

GEOWORDS
island
peninsula
tides
port

Know Virginia

1. The east coast of Virginia is known as the _____ .

2. The piedmont region in Virginia lies_____ of the Tidewater.

3. It is _____ in Virginia's mountains than in the state's lowland area.

4. Limestone _____ can be found under the Blue Ridge Mountains.

Map Study

1. Color the Chesapeake Bay and Atlantic Oceans blue.

2. Use dots to add in the cities of Virginia Beach, Roanoke, and Arlington. Label the cities.

3. Color Virginia's Appalachian Mountains brown. Color the piedmont region yellow.

4. Show on the map where coal is mined in Virginia.

5. Show on the map where fruit is grown in Virginia.

TENNESSEE ★ ★ ★ ★ ★ ★ ★ ★ ★ ★ ★ ★ ★ ★ ★ ★

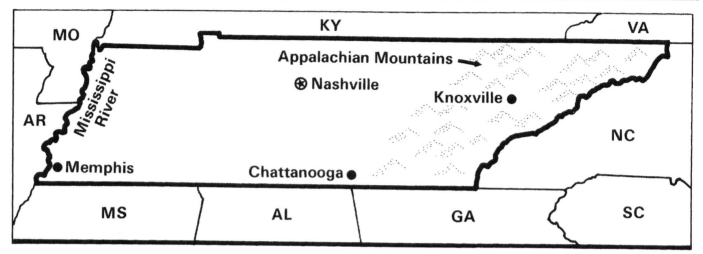

GEOFACTS
total area: 42,144 square miles
inland water: 989 square miles
population: 4,877,185
largest city: Memphis

GEOWORDS
earthquake
aftershock
steep
bluffs

Know Tennessee

1. Reelfoot Lake was formed by an ⎯⎯⎯⎯⎯⎯⎯⎯⎯⎯⎯⎯⎯⎯ .

2. Building a dam across a river can cause a ⎯⎯⎯⎯⎯⎯⎯⎯⎯ to form.

3. ⎯⎯⎯⎯⎯⎯⎯⎯ and ⎯⎯⎯⎯⎯⎯⎯⎯⎯ grow well in western Tennessee.

4. Dams built across the Tennessee River are used to make ⎯⎯⎯⎯⎯⎯⎯⎯⎯⎯⎯ .

Map Study

1. Trace the Mississippi River in blue. Then draw the Tennessee River in blue. Follow the full path of the Tennessee River.
2. Color the Appalachian Mountains brown.
3. Color the area covered by the Cherokee National Forest green.
4. Show on the map where corn is grown in Tennessee. Use a map symbol.
5. Use map symbols to show where four other farm crops are raised in Tennessee. Make a map key for all your symbols.

 Our United States Geography Workbook

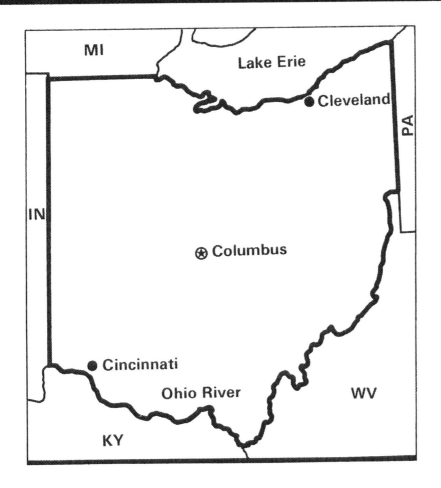

GEOFACTS
total area: 41,330 square miles
inland water: 326 square miles
population: 10,847,115
largest city: Columbus

GEOWORDS
foothills

Know Ohio

1. The Ohio River cuts across the —————————————— in western Ohio.

2. Ohio's snowbelt stretches across the state's —————————— region.

3. The ——————————forms a link between the Mississippi River and the Gulf of Mexico.

4. ———————————— and ———————————— are two of Ohio's major industries.

Map Study

1. Color Lake Erie blue. Use blue to trace the Ohio River.
2. Use dots to add the cities of Dayton, Canton, and Akron to the map. Label the cities.
3. Use green to color Ohio's Till Plain region. Use orange to color Ohio's Great Lakes Plains region. Use brown to color the Allegheny Plateau region.
4. Show six farm crops raised in Ohio by using map symbols.
5. Use map symbols to show four natural resources found in Ohio. Use your symbols to make a map key.

The Land Regions of the U.S. ★ ★ ★ ★ ★ ★ ★ ★

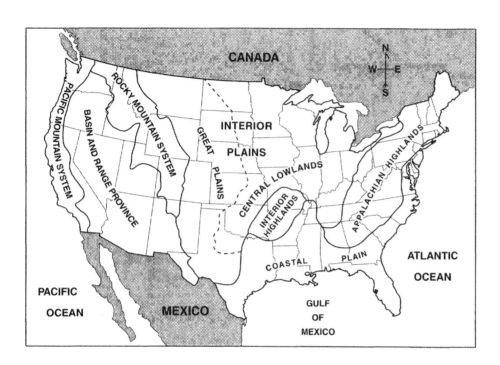

Map Study

1. Color the Pacific Ocean, Gulf of Mexico, Great Lakes, and Atlantic Ocean blue.
2. Color the Pacific Mountains, Rocky Mountains, and Appalachian Mountains brown.
3. Color the Great Plains yellow.
4. Color the Central Lowlands orange.
5. Color the Coastal Plain green.
6. Color American's Basin area tan.
7. Color the Interior Highlands red.

Fill in the blanks to tell the direction of the following land areas:

8. The Rocky Mountains run from the northwest to the _____ .
9. The Appalachian Mountains run from the northeast to the _____ .
10. The Coastal Plain runs along the _____ edge of the United States.

 Our United States Geography Workbook

The Northeast Corner

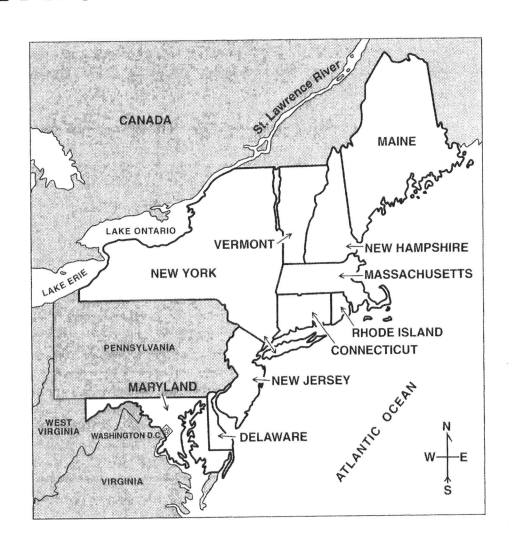

Map Study

1. Color the Atlantic Ocean, Great Lakes, and St. Lawrence River blue.
2. Color Canada red.
3. Draw lines show the direction of ocean currents along the Atlantic Coastline of the Northeast Corner states.

The Northeast Corner

Make a Graph!

List each state and its population. Then use the information to make a population bar graph. Make each bar 1/4" wide. Color each bar a different color. The state of Maryland has been done for you.

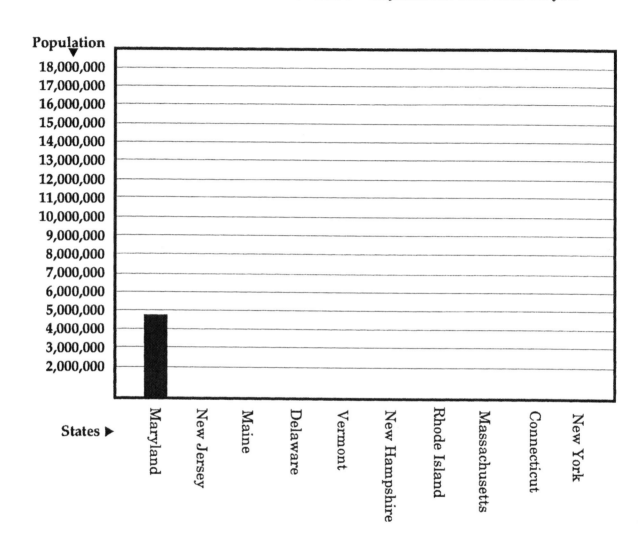

Population

18,000,000
17,000,000
16,000,000
15,000,000
14,000,000
13,000,000
12,000,000
11,000,000
10,000,000
9,000,000
8,000,000
7,000,000
6,000,000
5,000,000
4,000,000
3,000,000
2,000,000

States ▶

Maryland | New Jersey | Maine | Delaware | Vermont | New Hampshire | Rhode Island | Massachusetts | Connecticut | New York

 Spotlight

Patricia Harris (b. 1924) was the first African American woman to hold a cabinet post in the United States Government. In 1977, President Carter appointed Patricia Harris as secretary of housing and urban development. In 1979, President Carter appointed Harris as secretary of health, education, and welfare.

Before holding a cabinet post, Patricia Harris was a United States ambassador to Luxembourg (1965). She was also the first African American woman to head a major company in the United States (IBM).

 Our United States Geography Workbook

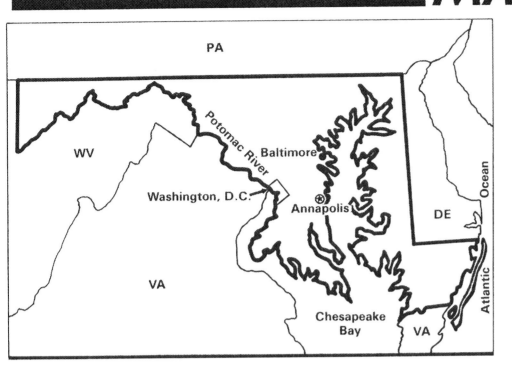

GEOFACTS
total area: 10,460 square miles
inland water: 623 square miles
population: 4,781,468
largest city: Baltimore

GEOWORDS
frontier
urban
canal

Know Maryland

1. During the early 1800s, people traveled west on the _____ .

2. Which mountains cross the northwest corner of Maryland? _____

3. Washington, D.C. is a district with its own _____ .

4. Washington, D.C. covers an area of _____ square miles.

Map Study

1. Use blue to trace the Potomac River. Then color the Chesapeake Bay and the Atlantic Ocean blue.

2. Color Maryland's coastal plain yellow.

3. Color Maryland's piedmont green.

4. Use your mountain symbol to add the Appalachian Mountains to the map. Label the mountains and color them brown.

5. Draw in route 95. Label the route.

NEW JERSEY

GEOFACTS
total area: 7,787 square miles
inland water: 319 square miles
population: 7,730,188
largest city: Newark

GEOWORDS
rural

Know New Jersey

1. Native Americans and Dutch immigrants once traded such things as _____

   and _____

2. New Jersey ranks _____ in population density.

3. _____ carved valleys in northern New Jersey.

4. New Jersey's lowland region rises about _____ feet above sea level.

Map Study

1. Use blue to trace the Delaware River. Color Delaware Bay and the Atlantic Ocean blue.
2. Color the Atlantic Coastal Plain yellow. Color the piedmont green.
3. Color the New England Upland orange. Color the Appalachian mountain area red.
4. Add the New Jersey turnpike to the map. Label the turnpike.
5. Add the Garden State Parkway to the map. Label the road.

   Our United States Geography Workbook

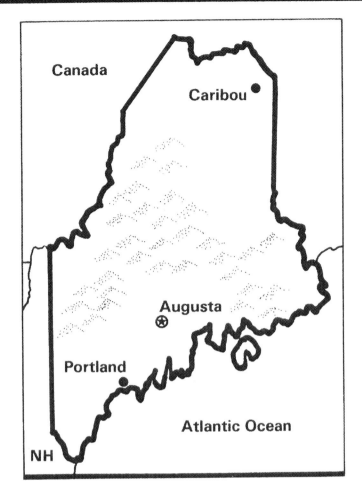

GEOFACTS
total area: 33,265 square miles
inland water: 2,270 square miles
population: 1,227,928
largest city: Portland

GEOWORDS
dawn
stream
marsh
spring
acre

Know Maine

1. Pine _____ cover most of Maine.

2. What crop is most often grown across the Arrostook Plateau?_____

3. Long gravel mountain rides are called _____

4. _____ and _____ keep Maine colder than other areas found

   as far north as Maine.

Map Study

1. Color the Atlantic Ocean blue.
2. Add Moosehead Lake to the map. Color it blue.
3. Use your mountain peak symbol to show where White Cap mountain is found. Label the mountain.
4. Show where route 95 crosses the state. Label the route.
5. Use dots to add the cities of Bangor, Waterville, and Rockland to the map. Label the cities.

DELAWARE ★ ★ ★ ★ ★ ★ ★ ★ ★ ★ ★ ★ ★ ★ ★ ★ ★

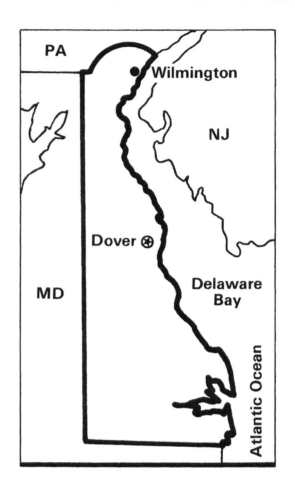

GEOFACTS
  total area: 2,044 square miles
  inland water: 112 square miles
  population: 666,168
  largest city: Wilmington

GEOWORDS
  refuge

Know Delaware

1. Delaware was the first state to pass a law to protect the right to _____ and

   to allow _____ .

2. Delaware is the only state that divides counties into _____ .

3. _____ covers a small part of northern Delaware.

4. Most of Delaware's land is part of the _____ .

Map Study

1. Color the Atlantic Ocean and Delaware Bay blue.
2. Color the Coastal Plain region yellow. Color the piedmont region green.
3. Use dots to add the cities of New Castle, Milford, Middleton, and Rehoboth Beach to the map. Label the cities.
4. Add route 95 to the map. Label the route.
5. Trace all the route that runs south from Dover to the Delaware-Maryland border. Label the route.

 Our United States Geography Workbook

VERMONT

★ ★ ★ ★ ★ ★ ★ ★ ★ ★ ★ ★ ★ ★ ★ ★ ★

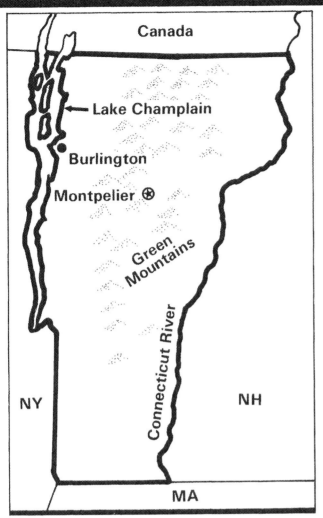

GEOFACTS
total area: 9,614 square miles
inland water: 341 square miles
population: 562,758
largest city: Burlington

GEOWORDS
range
quarry
pond

Know Vermont

1. Vermont is a state of _____ towns with populations of under 2,500 people.

2. Many of Vermont's lakes and ponds were formed from a _____ that covered the state long ago.

3. _____ and _____ areas cover much of Vermont.

4. Rivers starting high in the Green Mountains flow either east to the _____ or west to _____ .

Map Study

1. Trace the Connecticut River in blue. Then color Lake Champlain blue.

2. Color the area of the White Mountains brown. Label the mountains.

3. Color the area covered by the Green Mountains tan.

4. Add route 91 to the map. Label the route.

5. Add the route that runs between Burlington and Montpelier. Label the route.

NEW HAMPSHIRE ★ ★ ★ ★ ★ ★ ★ ★ ★ ★ ★

GEOFACTS
total area: 9,279 square miles
inland water: 286 square miles
population: 1,109,252
largest city: Manchester

GEOWORDS
seasons .
meadows

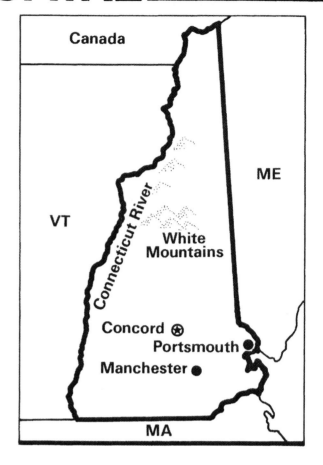

Know New Hampshire

1. New Hampshire's three main land regions are the _____ _____ .

2. What special landmark is found in the White Mountains? _____

3. The White Mountains are part of the _____ chain.

4. New Hampshire is the first state in the country to hold a _____ election for president of the United States.

Map Study

1. Trace the Connecticut River in blue. Color the Atlantic Ocean in blue.
2. Color the Coastal Lowland region in yellow.
3. Use green to show the area covered by White Mountain National Park.
4. Add route 95 to the map. Label the route.
5. Add route 93 to the map. Use dots to add three cities route 93 crosses. Label the cities.

 Our United States Geography Workbook

RHODE ISLAND

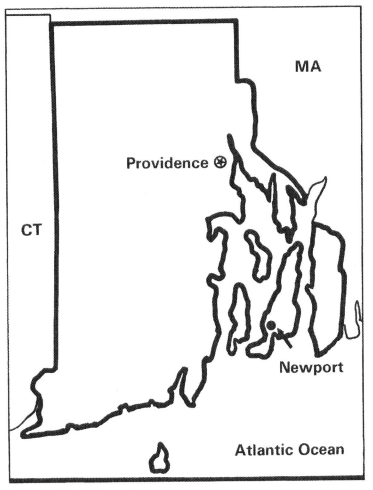

GEOFACTS

total area: 1,212 square miles
inland water: 157 square miles
population: 1,003,464
largest city: Providence

GEOWORDS

lagoons

Know Rhode Island

1. What kind of factory was built in Rhode Island in the early 1800s? _____

2. In size, Rhode Island is the _____ of all the states.

3. Many small _____ can be found along Rhode Island's coast.

4. The two land regions that form Rhode Island are _____ and

_____ .

Map Study

1. Color the Atlantic Ocean blue.
2. Color Narrangansett Bay blue. Label the bay.
3. Use blue to add the Wood River, Pautuxet River, and Ponaganset River to the map. Label each river.
4. Add route 95 to the map. Label the route.
5. Add routes 102 and 1 to the map. Label each map.

Our United States Geography Workbook

MASSACHUSETTS ★ ★ ★ ★ ★ ★ ★ ★ ★ ★

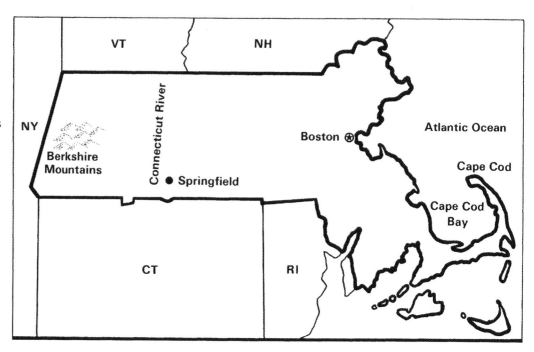

GEOFACTS

total area: 8,284 square miles
inland water: 460 square miles
population: 6,016,425
largest city: Boston

GEOWORDS

countryside
cape
sound
surf

Know Massachusetts

1. Massachusetts is also called the _____ state.

2. Massachusetts has about _____ miles of coastline.

3. Nantucket Sound and Martha's Vineyard are important to the _____ economy of Massachusetts.

4. _____ , _____ , and _____ are found across the state's coastal lowland region.

Map Study

1. Use blue to add the Connecticut River to the map. Then color the Atlantic Ocean and Cape Cod Bay blue.

2. Color the Coastal Lowland yellow. Color the Uplands green.

3. Use dots to add the cities of Worchester, New Bedford, and Pittsfield to the map. Label each city.

4. Add route 95 to the map. Label the route.

5. Add the route that runs from Springfield to Boston. Label the route.

 Our United States Geography Workbook

★ ★ ★ ★ ★ ★ ★ ★ ★ ★ CONNECTICUT

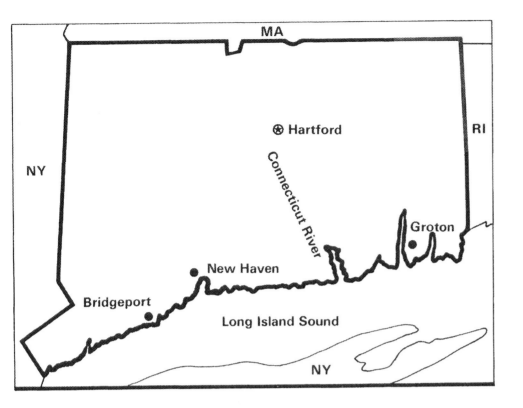

GEOFACTS

total area: 5,018 square miles
inland water: 146 square miles
population: 3,287,116
largest city: Bridgeport

GEOWORDS

ravine
ridge

Know Connecticut

1. _____ , _____ , and _____

   are some of the crops that grow in Connecticut's central valley.

2. The soil of Connecticut's New England upland is _____ and

   _____ .

3. Along the western edge of Connecticut are found the _____ .

4. Connecticut's climate is filled with many _____ .

Map Study

1. Trace the Connecticut River in blue. Then color Long Island Sound in blue.
2. Use dots to add the cities of Bridgeport, Waterbury, and Winsted to the map. Label the cities.
3. Add route 95 to the map. Label the route.
4. Add in a route that can be taken from Hartford to Thompsonville. Label the route.
5. Add a route that can be taken from Winsted to Waterbury. Label the route.

Our United States Geography Workbook

NEW YORK ★ ★ ★ ★ ★ ★ ★ ★ ★ ★ ★ ★ ★ ★ ★ ★

GEOFACTS

total area: 49,108 square miles
inland water: 1,713 square miles
population: 17,990,445
largest city: New York

GEOWORDS

palisades
cliffs

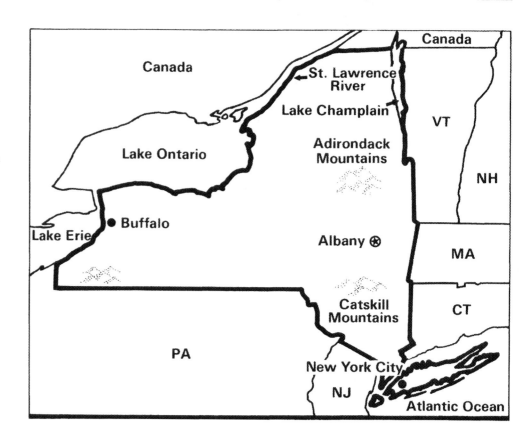

Know New York

1. Cities north of New York City have _____ summers and _____

   winters than New York city.

2. Great _____ are found along the Hudson River.

3. Each year, about 15 million people travel to New York to see the _____.

4. The state of New York touches both the _____ and the

   _____ .

Map Study

1. Color Lake Ontario, Lake Erie, the St. Lawrence River, and the Atlantic Ocean blue.
2. Use your mountain peaks symbol to show where Mt. Marcy is found in New York. Label the mountain. Write its height under the label.
3. Use blue to add the Hudson River to the map. Label the river.
4. Add the cities of Niagara Falls, Syracuse, and Utica to the map. Label the cities.
5. Add the route that goes from Buffalo to Syracuse to Albany. Label the route.

 Our United States Geography Workbook

Map Study

1. Color the Great Lakes blue.
2. Using blue, draw in the Mississippi River from its start in Minnesota to the bottom of the map. Label the River.
3. Color the country that borders the Great Lakes states red.
4. Using a dotted line, show where the Canada-United States border lies across the Great Lakes.
5. Color the state of Michigan orange.

The Heartland ★★★★★★★★★★★★★★★

GeoThoughts

Find out where the following cities are:

Chicago

St. Louis

Milwaukee

Detroit

Dubuque

Gary

St. Paul

Add each city to the map. Show how far the city extends by shading the area covered by the city. Label each city.

Look at where each city is found. You should see a pattern to where cities grow to become large cities. Explain this pattern. Tell WHY you think each city grew to become a large city. Give at least three reasons for the pattern you see.

_____

_____

_____

_____

_____

_____

_____

 ## Spotlight

Golda Meir was born in 1893 in Ukraine. Her family moved to Milwaukee, Wisconsin, where she later taught school. In 1921, Golda Meir traveled far across the Atlantic Ocean to Palestine. There she joined a collective farm community. After World War II, part of Palestine became the country of Israel. Golda Meir became Israel's first woman prime minister in 1969.

Our United States Geography Workbook

WISCONSIN

GEOFACTS
total area: 56,153 square miles
inland water: 1,727 square miles
population: 4,891,769
largest city: Milwaukee

GEOWORDS
mineral
prairie

Know Wisconsin

1. Wisconsin is a leading state in such dairy products as _____ ,

_____ , and _____ .

2. The making of _____ products is one of Wisconsin's leading industries.

3. Spreading over half of Wisconsin are lush _____ of pine, birch and oak.

4. More than 20,000 miles of _____ and 15,000

_____ can be found in Wisconsin.

Map Study

1. Trace the Mississippi River in blue. Then color Lake Superior and Lake Michigan blue.
2. Use dots to add the cities of Eau Claire, Wausau, Racine, and La Crosse to the map. Label each city.
3. Add Lake Winnebago to the map. Label the lake.
4. Add the river that flows from Lake Winnebago to Green Bay. Label the river.
5. Color Wisconsin's forest areas green.

ILLINOIS

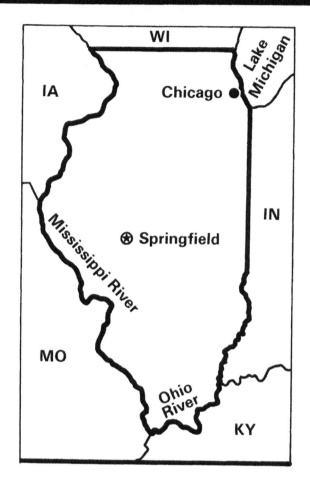

GEOFACTS
total area: 56,345 square miles
inland water: 700 square miles
population: 11,430,602
largest city: Chicago

GEOWORDS
regionalism

Know Illinois

1. The city of Chicago began as a trading post owned by a man named _____

   _____ .

2. The rolling hills of northern Illinois were carved by _____ many years ago.

3. Across southern Illinois stretch the _____ Hills.

4. _____ and _____ are two farm crops grown in

   central Illinois.

Map Study

1. Trace the Ohio River and the Mississippi River in blue. Color Lake Michigan blue.
2. Using blue, add the Rock River, Illinois River, Kaskaskia River, Big Muddy River, and Fox River to the map. Label each river.
3. Color the area covered by the Shawnee Hills brown.
4. Color the Great Lakes plains region yellow.
5. Color the Till Plains region green.

 Our United States Geography Workbook

GEOFACTS
total area: 36,185 square miles
inland water: 253 square miles
population: 5,544,159
largest city: Indianapolis

GEOWORDS
caverns
shallow

Know Indiana

1. Indiana's three land regions are _____
   _____ .

2. Limestone_____ can be found in southern Indiana.

3. Why was the city of Gary, Indiana, started? _____
   _____

4. Most of Indiana's forests are found in the _____ part of the
   state.

Map Study

1. Use blue to trace the Ohio River and Wabash River. Color Lake Michigan blue.
2. Using blue, add Indiana's four largest lakes to the map. Label each lake.
3. Using blue, add the river that flows from Monroe Lake to the Wabash River.
4. Color Indiana's Sand Dunes area yellow.
5. Find out which hill in Indiana rises 1,058 feet above sea level. Mark and then label the hill on the map.

MINNESOTA

★ ★ ★ ★ ★ ★ ★ ★ ★ ★ ★ ★ ★ ★ ★

GEOFACTS
total area: 84,402 square miles
inland water: 4,854 square miles
population: 4,375,099
largest city: Minneapolis

GEOWORDS
moraines
till

Know Minnesota

1. The Homestead Act gave the head of a family _____ acres of free land.

2. The _____ region covers most of northern and eastern Minnesota.

3. The Mississippi River gets its start from Lake _____ .

4. _____ is fertile soil left by the glaciers that covered Minnesota long ago.

Map Study

1. Find where the Mississippi River begins in Minnesota. Trace the Mississippi River in blue. Color Lake Superior in blue.

2. Color Minnesota's Superior Upland region yellow.

3. Color Minnesota's Young Drift Plain region orange.

4. Choose four rivers to add to the map. Draw the rivers in blue. Label each river.

5. Using blue, add four lakes to the map. Label each lake.

 Our United States Geography Workbook

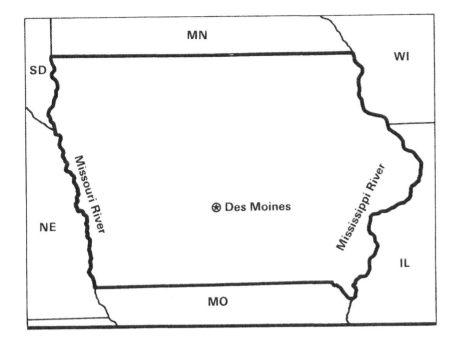

GEOFACTS
total area: 56,275 square miles
inland water: 310 square miles
population: 2,776,755
largest city: Des Moines

GEOWORDS
sod
drought

Know Iowa

1. Early white emigrants in Iowa used _____ to build homes.

2. About 90% of Iowa is _____ .

3. The fertile soil that lines the valleys of Iowa was brought there long ago by _____ .

4. Many of Iowa's largest lakes were made by _____ built across rivers.

Map Study

1. Use blue to trace the Missouri River and Mississippi River.
2. Using blue, add the Iowa River, Des Moines River, and Little Sioux River to the map. Label each river.
3. Using dots, add the cities of Sioux City, Ft. Dodge, Cedar Rapids, Dubuque, and Davenport to the map. Label each city.
4. Color the Missouri River Valley brown.
5. Color the Mississippi River Valley orange.

Our United States Geography Workbook

MISSOURI

★ ★ ★ ★ ★ ★ ★ ★ ★ ★ ★ ★ ★ ★ ★ ★

GEOFACTS
total area: 69,697 square miles
inland water: 752 square miles
population: 5,117,073
largest city: Kansas City

GEOWORDS
deserts

Know Missouri

1. What earth force formed the area around Hannibal, Missouri? _____

2. Soybeans and corn easily grow in the _____ soil of Missouri's Till

   Plains region.

3. Over 1,400 limestone _____ can be found in Missouri.

4. The _____ land between the Rocky Mountains and Appalachian Mountains

   is found in the region of Missouri.

Map Study

1. Trace the Missouri River and Mississippi River in blue.
2. Use your mountain peak symbol to add Taum Sauk Mountain, Thorny Mountain, and Long Mountain to the map. Label each mountain. Write the height of each mountain under the label.
3. Using blue, add two rivers that flow into the Mississippi River. Label each river.
4. Using blue, add three rivers that flow into the Missouri River. Label each river.
5. Color the Ozark region yellow.

 Our United States Geography Workbook

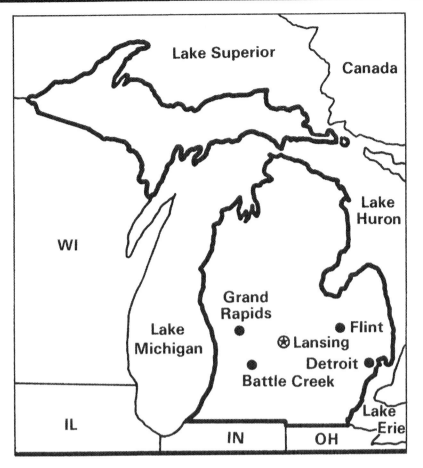

GEOFACTS
total area: 58,527 square miles
inland water: 1,573 square miles
population: 9,295,297
largest city: Detroit

GEOWORDS
woods

Know Michigan

1. Michigan has been a good place to build cars because it is rich in the natural resources of

_____ and _____ .

2. Michigan is rich in the natural resource of water, and often is called a "_____

_____ ."

3. Michigan is divided into an _____ peninsula and a _____ peninsula.

4. Michigan's farmland is found across the _____ Peninsula.

Map Study

1. Color the Great Lakes blue.

2. Label Michigan's Upper Peninsula. Label Michigan's Lower Peninsula.

3. Think of a map symbol for a forest area. Use your symbol to show where most of Michigan's forest areas are found.

4. Label Green Bay and Saginaw Bay.

5. Using brown, add the Beaver Islands to the map. Label the islands.

Our United States Environment

The Great Flood of '93

The following information tells the cresting point of the Mississippi River at points along the river. A river's crest is the highest level reached by floodwaters. Plot each city on the map.

Label each city and its cresting point.

Davenport, Iowa - 22 feet, 6 inches
Jefferson City, Missouri - 38 feet
St. Paul, Minnesota - 19 feet, 2 inches
St. Louis, Missouri - 49 feet

Kansas City, Missouri - 36 feet, 8 inches
Des Moines, Iowa - 34 feet, 3 inches
Cairo, Illinois - 45 feet, 5 inches

1. Look at the crests recorded for each city. What can you say about the floodwaters as they traveled southward? _____

_____

_____

2. Many people returned to their homes after the floodwaters had gone only to find their homes badly damaged or no longer there. _____

Explain three problems these people faced. _____

_____

_____

_____

 Our United States Geography Workbook

Hurricane Andrew

A timeline shows what happened at certain points in time. It is divided into equal points in time. For example, a timeline might divide the last one hundred years into blocks of ten years each. Then the date of each damaging hurricane for the last one hundred years could be noted in the correct block.

Make a timeline for Hurricane Andrew. First draw a line from one side of the page to the other. Look at the times noted on the map. Divide your line into equal blocks of time. Plot the map times and wind speeds on your timeline.

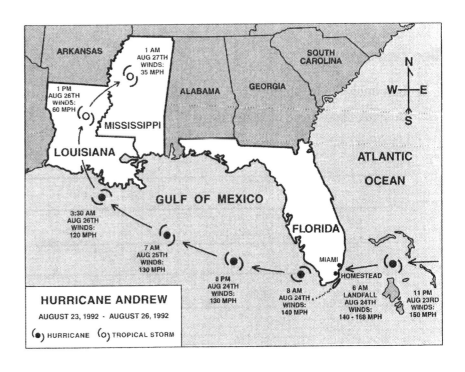

The Great Plains

GeoThoughts

1. List each Great Plains state. Write the state's total land area next to the state. Then rewrite the states in order from largest to smallest.

STATE	TOTAL LAND AREA	RANK IN SIZE

2. List each Great Plains state. Write the state's inland water area next to the state. Then rewrite the states in order from most inland water to the least amount.

STATE	TOTAL INLAND WATER	RANK IN AMOUNT

3. List each Great Plains state. Write the state's population next to the state. Then rewrite the states in order from greatest population to least population.

STATE	POPULATION	RANK IN POPULATION

4. Which state has the greatest total area? _____ the least? _____

5. Which state has the greatest amount of inland water? _____

    the least amount? _____

6. Which state has the largest population? _____ the smallest? _____

_____

 ## Spotlight

Bill Pickett (b. 1860) is famous for having invented rodeo steer wrestling. In the rodeo, steer wrestling is called "bulldogging." Bill Pickett is one of several African American cowboys who rode the cow trails during the 1800's. Bill Pickett was a star in early 1900 silent films. Bill Pickett became the first African American voted into Oklahoma City's Cowboy Hall of Fame in 1971.

NORTH DAKOTA ★ ★ ★ ★ ★ ★ ★ ★ ★ ★

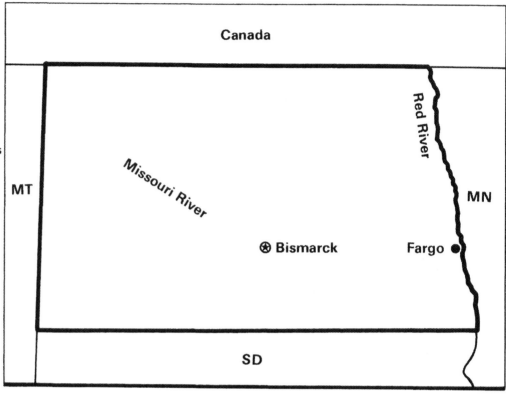

GEOFACTS

total area: 70,703 square miles
inland water: 1,403 square miles
population: 638,800
largest city: Fargo

GEOWORDS

buttes
reservation

Know North Dakota

1. In the southwest part of North Dakota, gently sloping hills called _____

   can be found.

2. Lignite is found in a treeless region of North Dakota called the _____.

3. Turtle Mountains are found in North Dakota's forest region called the _____.

4. _____ left rich soil across North Dakota's Red River Valley.

Map Study

1. Trace the Red River in blue. Draw the Missouri River in blue. Use blue to add Lake Sakakawea to the map. Label the lake and the river.

2. Color the Red River Valley area green. Label the area.

3. Color the Badlands brown. Label the area.

4. Use your mountain symbol to add the Turtle Mountains to the map. Label the mountains.

5. Find out where Garrison Dam and Baldhill Dam are found. Think of a symbol for a dam. Add the two dams to the map. Label the dams.

 Our United States Geography Workbook

SOUTH DAKOTA

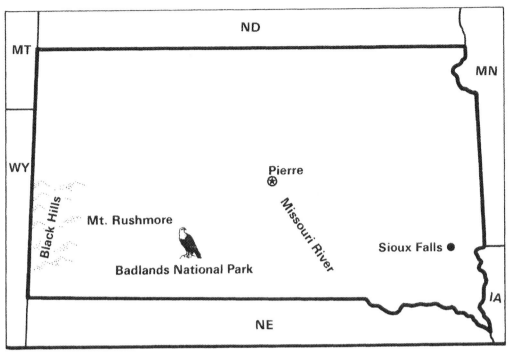

GEOFACTS
total area: 77,116 square miles
inland water: 1,164 square miles
population: 696,004
largest city: Sioux Falls

GEOWORDS
range

Know South Dakota

1. South Dakota's two main land regions are divided by the _____River.

2. The_____ Hills are found in the western part of the state.

3. South Dakota's Badlands lie between the _____ River and

   the _____ River.

4. South Dakota's leading farm crops are _____ and _____ .

Map Study

1. Using blue, add the Missouri River to the map.
2. Use your mountain symbol to add the Black Hills to the map. Label the Black Hills.
3. Put a circle on the map to show where the geographic center of the United States is found. Label this point.
4. Use blue to add the Cheyenne and White Rivers to the map. Label each river.
5. Color the Badlands National Park area tan.

NEBRASKA

GEOFACTS

total area: 77,335 square miles
inland water: 711 square miles
population: 1,578,385
largest city: Omaha

GEOWORDS

groundwater
irrigation

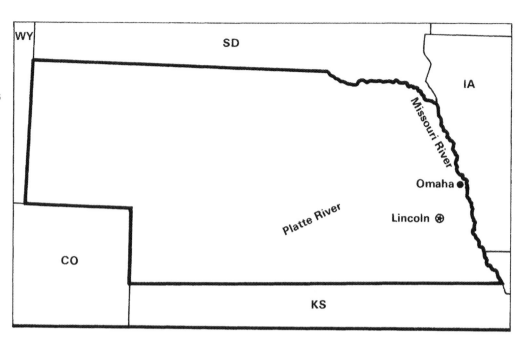

Know Nebraska

1. Nebraska land rises about _____ feet for each mile when traveling from east to west.

2. Rolling hills of _____ cover Nebraska's Great Plains region.

3. Only about _____ inches of rain falls in western Nebraska each year, while about _____ inches of rain falls in eastern Nebraska.

4. Over half of Nebraska's land is drained by the _____.

Map Study

1. Trace the Missouri River in blue. Using blue, add the Platte River to the map. Add five rivers that flow into the Platte River. Label each river.

2. Color Nebraska's Sand Hills region in yellow.

3. Using blue, add Lewis and Clark Lake. Label the lake.

4. Find out where Hogback Mountain is found. Use your mountain peak symbol to place Hogback Mountain on the map. Label the mountain.

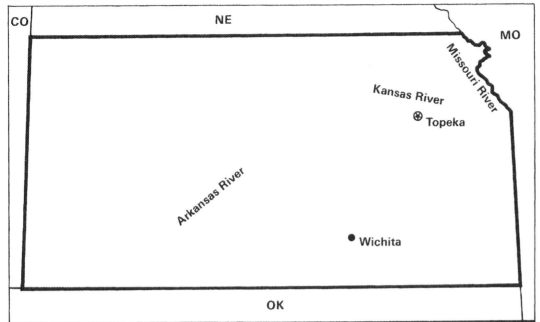

GEOFACTS
total area: 82,227 square miles
inland water: 499 square miles
population: 2,477,574
largest city: Wichita

GEOWORDS
spires
brush

Know Kansas

1. Some people call Kansas the "_____ State."

2. _____ covers the state of Kansas.

3. Tall bluffs of rock called _____ are found in the northwest part

   of the state.

4. All rivers in Kansas flow _____ .

Map Study

1. Trace the Missouri River in blue. Using blue, add the Kansas River and the Arkansas River to the map.
2. Use blue to add the following lakes to the map: Wilson, Perry, Milford, and Elk City. Label each lake.
3. Think of a railroad symbol for your map. Use your symbol to add the Chicago Rock Island and Pacific Railroad and the Missouri Pacific Railroad lines to the map. Label the railroad lines.
4. Color the Smoky Hills brown.
5. Color the Sand Hills yellow.

OKLAHOMA

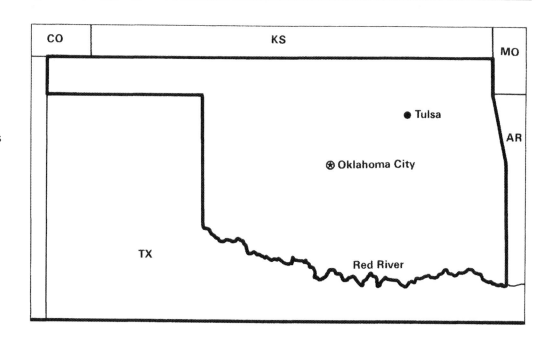

GEOFACTS
total area: 69,956 square miles
inland water: 1,301 square miles
population: 3,145,585
largest city: Oklahoma City

GEOWORDS
mesa

Know Oklahoma

1. Oklahoma tilts from _____ to _____.

2. Most of Oklahoma's lakes are found in the _____ part of the state.

3. Oklahoma is a leading state in the raising of _____.

4. About _____ inches of rain fall in the southeast part of the state while only about

   _____ inches fall in Oklahoma's Panhandle.

Map Study

1. Trace the Red River in blue.

2. Use blue to add the Canadian River and the Arkansas River to the map. Label each river.

3. Place a red dot on the map to show where the Black Mesa is found. Label the area. Write the elevation under the label.

4. Using dots, show where the cities of Wagoner, Hog Shooter, Broken Arrow, and Oil City are found in Oklahoma. Label each city.

5. Color Oklahoma's Panhandle orange.

 Our United States Geography Workbook

The Climate of the U.S.

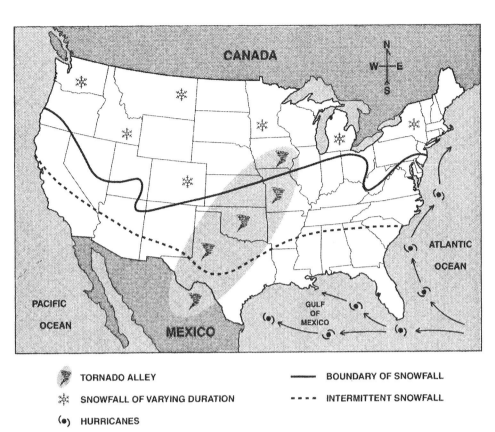

TORNADO ALLEY

SNOWFALL OF VARYING DURATION

(•) HURRICANES

—— **BOUNDARY OF SNOWFALL**

- - - - **INTERMITTENT SNOWFALL**

Map Study

1. Color the area where snow is sure to fall white.

2. Color the area where snow may or may not fall during the cold months of the year green.

3. Color the area of the United States that rarely gets snow brown.

4. Trace the coastline most likely to be affected by hurricanes in red.

5. Color the area most often affected by tornadoes gray.

Think of the climate across the United States. Then answer the next two questions.

6. Which area of the United States would you most like to live in? _____

   Give at least two reasons why: _____

   _____

7. Which area of the United States would you least like to live in? _____

   Give at least two reasons why: _____

   _____

The Rocky Mountains

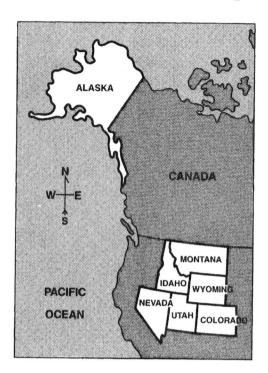

Make a Graph!

You will need to use your mountain symbol for this activity.

Each mountain symbol will equal 50,000 square miles. Draw in one mountain symbol after another in a row to show the total square miles of land area. The first state has been done for you.

ALASKA	△	△	△	△	△	△	△	△	△	△	△	△
MONTANA												
WYOMING												
COLORADO												
IDAHO												
UTAH												
NEVADA												

 Our United States Geography Workbook

Map Study

1. Use your mountain symbol to show the line of the Rocky Mountains from Alaska to south of Utah.
2. Color the Pacific Ocean blue.
3. Color the Arctic Ocean blue. Label the ocean.
4. Use red to trace over the line which shows the border between Canada and the United States.

 Spotlight

Florence Rena Sabin became the first woman to be elected to the National Academy of Science. Born in 1871 in Central City, Colorado, Florence Rena Sabin studied, and then taught, at Johns Hopkins University School of Medicine. Sabin became famous for her work in public health. Her statue, representing the state of Colorado, stands in the United States Capitol.

ALASKA

★ ★ ★ ★ ★ ★ ★ ★ ★ ★ ★ ★ ★ ★ ★ ★ ★ ★ ★

GEOFACTS

total area: 591,004 square miles
inland water: 20,171 square miles
population: 550,043
largest city: Anchorage

GEOWORDS

glacier
permafrost

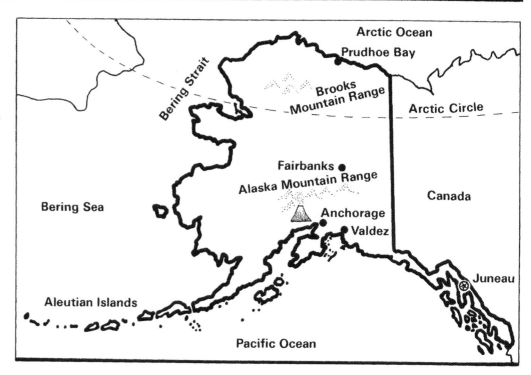

Know Alaska

1. Over _____ of all the people living in Alaska settled there from other places

   outside of the state.

2. _____ covers the ground of northern Alaska.

3. The land bridge crossed by Native Americans many thousand years ago today can be found under the

   _____ .

4. The discovery of _____ has brought both riches and problems to Alaska.

Map Study

1. Color the Pacific Ocean, Arctic Ocean, and Bering Sea blue.
2. Color the Brooks Mountain Range brown.
3. Color the Aleutian Islands orange.
4. Color the Alaska Range tan.
5. Find out how far it is from the western edge of Alaska to the eastern edge of Russia. Write the number
   of miles on your map.

 Our United States Geography Workbook

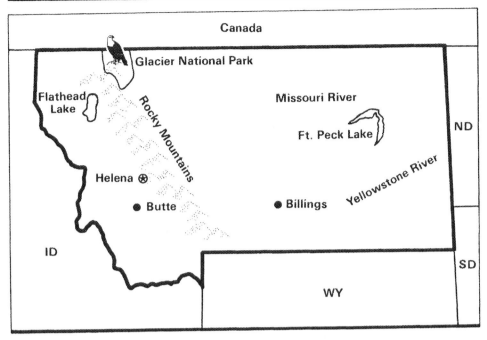

GEOFACTS
total area: 147,046 square miles
inland water: 1,658 square miles
population: 799,065
largest city: Billings

GEOWORDS
gulch

Know Montana

1. Montana's two land regions are the _____ to the east and

   the _____ to the west.

2. Over _____ mountain ranges stretch across Montana.

3. Montana's climate is affected by the _____ .

4. Because of the Rocky Mountains, more rain falls in _____ Montana

   than in eastern Montana.

Map Study

1. Using blue, add the Missouri River and the Yellowstone River to the map. Color Flathead Lake and Fort Peck Lake blue.

2. Color the area of the Rocky Mountains brown.

3. Color the area of greatest rainfall yellow.

4. Think of a snow symbol. Add the snow symbol to the map to show where snow falls most often in Montana.

5. Using blue, add the Big Horn River and the Little Big Horn River to the map. Label each river.

WYOMING

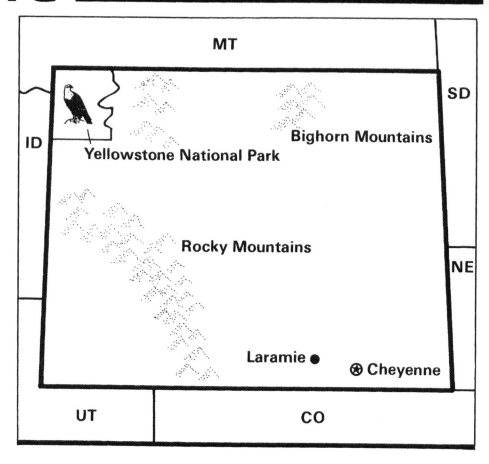

GEOFACTS

total area: 97,809 square miles
inland water: 820 square miles
population: 453,588
largest city: Cheyenne

GEOWORDS

geyser
canyon
gap

Know Wyoming

1. _____ form near rivers or lakes where water drains into the earth.

2. Which region covers the eastern part of Wyoming? _____

3. The Continental Divide splits around Wyoming's _____ .

4. Wyoming can get up to _____ of snow in one year in its mountain area.

Map Study

1. Color the area covered by the Yellowstone National Park green.

2. Using blue, add Yellowstone Lake to the map. Label the lake.

3. Color the area covered by the Rocky Mountains brown.

4. Use your snow symbol to show which area of Montana has the greatest amount of snowfall.

5. Color the Great Plains area orange.

 Our United States Geography Workbook

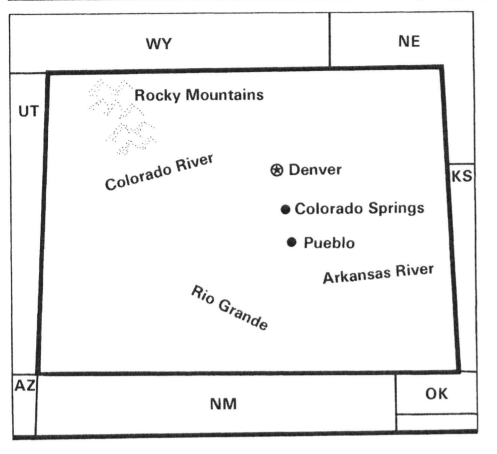

GEOFACTS
total area: 104,091 square miles
inland water: 496 square miles
population: 3,294,394
largest city: Denver

GEOWORDS
lode

Know Colorado

1. Colorado's Great Plains region lies along the _____ part of the state.

2. Farming is no longer allowed in the _____ and the _____ .

3. Some Rocky Mountain peaks stretch to a height of _____ feet above sea level.

4. _____ is used to change the dry plain into fertile farmland.

Map Study

1. Using blue, add the Colorado River, the Rio Grande River, and the Arkansas River to the map.

2. Color the area of the Rocky Mountains brown. Add more mountain symbols to the map to show the whole area.

3. Color the Great Plains region yellow.

4. Using blue, add the South Platte River to the map. Label the river.

5. Find out where the San Luis Valley is found. Color the valley green.

IDAHO

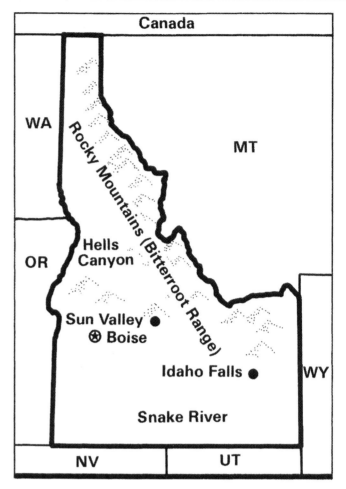

GEOFACTS

total area: 83,564 square miles
inland water: 1,152 square miles
population: 1,006,749
largest city: Boise

GEOWORDS

current
wasteland

Know Idaho

1. Idaho's ―――――――――― affects its climate.

2. Rainfall along the Snake River averages about ―――――――――― inches each year.

3. Forests cover about ―――――――――― of Idaho's land.

4. Irrigation has changed dry ―――――――――― into fertile farming areas.

Map Study

1. Using blue add the Snake River to Idaho. Show where the Snake River travels beyond Idaho's borders.
2. Color the area covered by the Rocky Mountains brown.
3. Color the area of Idaho that gets the least amount of rain yellow.
4. Draw a square on the map to show where Craters of the Moon National Monument is found in Idaho. Label this place of interest.
5. Find out where the Nez Perce National Park is found. Label this area on the map.

 Our United States Geography Workbook

UTAH

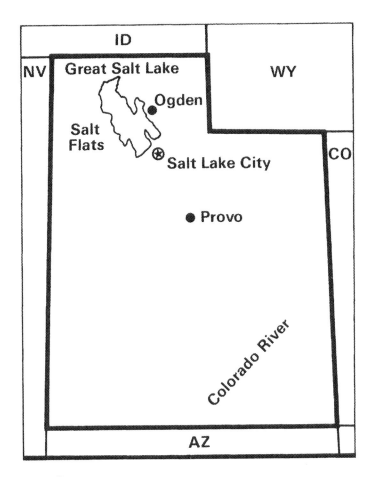

GEOFACTS
total area: 84,889 square miles
inland water: 2,826 square miles
population: 1,722,850
largest city: Salt Lake City

GEOWORDS
stalactites
stalagmites

Know Utah

1. Both _____ and _____ can be found deep in limestone caves.

2. The _____ covers the western third of Utah.

3. Salt Lake is found in the _____ corner of the Great Basin.

4. Concrete hard _____ can be found across the Great Salt Lake Desert.

Map Study

1. Use blue to add the Colorado River to the map. Show where the river extends into other states.

2. Use blue to color the Great Salt Lake. Use blue to add Utah Lake and Sevier Lake to the map. Label each lake.

3. Color the Great Basin yellow.

4. Use your map symbol to show where the Rocky Mountains cross Utah. Label the mountains and color them brown.

5. Color the Great Salt Lake Desert orange. Label this desert area.

NEVADA

★ ★ ★ ★ ★ ★ ★ ★ ★ ★ ★ ★ ★ ★ ★ ★ ★ ★ ★ ★

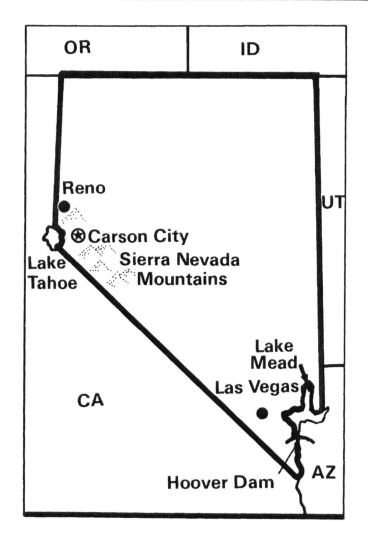

GEOFACTS

total area: 110,561 square miles
inland water: 667 square miles
population: 1,201,883
largest city: Las Vegas

GEOWORDS

outlets
sinks

Know Nevada

1. At one time, long ago in the history of the earth, Nevada was covered by _____ .

2. Most of Nevada's rivers only flow during times of _____ .

3. Most of Nevada gets only about _____ of rain each year.

4. Nevada's largest industry is _____ .

Map Study

1. Use blue to color Lake Mead and Lake Tahoe. Then use blue to add the Humboldt River to the map. Label the river.

2. Use your mountain symbol to show where the Haystack Mountains are found. Color the mountains brown and label them.

3. Color the Great Basin yellow.

4. Find out where Nevada's highest peak, Boundary Peak, is found. Label this point. Write its elevation.

5. Color the Sierra Nevada Mountains tan.

 Our United States Geography Workbook

The Southwest

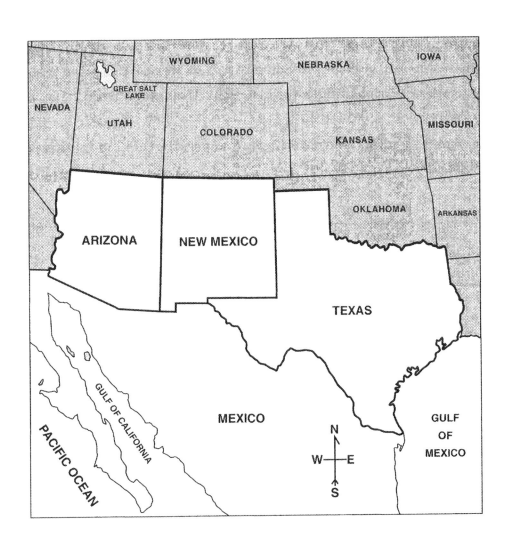

Map Study

1. Color Mexico orange.
2. Color the Pacific Ocean, the Gulf of Mexico, and the Gulf of California blue.
3. Use blue to draw in the Colorado River showing how it travels across state borders. Label the river.
4. Use blue to add the Rio Grande River. Label the river.
5. Use a star to show where the capital of each state of the Southwest region is found. Label each city.

The Southwest

GeoThoughts

Using red, add the Gila Trail to the map (see workbook page 70). Use blue to add Route 25 in New Mexico. Find where Route 10 branches off Route 25 in New Mexico. Use green to show where Route 10 crosses New Mexico to where it meets with Route 8 in Arizona. Use orange to add in Route 8 from Arizona to the California border.

Look carefully at what you have drawn. Compare the Gila Trail with present routes traveled today. What do you notice?

_____

_____

_____

_____

_____

_____

 Spotlight

Henry Cisneros became the first Mexican American to be elected as mayor of a large United States city (San Antonio, Texas, 1981). Cisneros was born in San Antonio, Texas in 1947. He received degrees from Harvard University and George Washington University. He was first elected to San Antonio's city council in 1975. He was elected two more times before becoming mayor.

 Our United States Geography Workbook

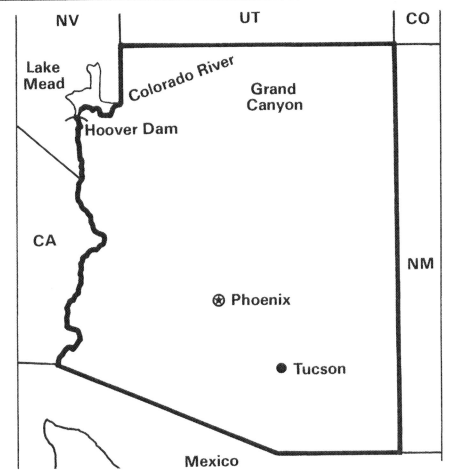

GEOFACTS
total area: 114,000 square miles
inland water: 492 square miles
population: 3,665,228
largest city: Phoenix

GEOWORDS
adobe
arid

Know Arizona

1. The Grand Canyon has been shaped by both_____ and _____.

2. Arizona is a dry state with most areas getting about _____inches of rain each

   year.

3. Much of Arizona's land is used for grazing _____ and

   _____.

4. Arizona is a leading state in the mining of _____ .

Map Study

1. Use blue to add the Colorado River to the map. Show where the river extends into other states.

2. Color the Grand Canyon shades of orange and brown.

3. Use blue to add the Gila River and the Little Colorado River to the map. Label the river.

4. Color Arizona's areas of high elevation green. Color the areas of low elevation yellow.

5. Color the painted desert shades of pink, yellow, and tan.

NEW MEXICO ★ ★ ★ ★ ★ ★ ★ ★ ★ ★ ★ ★ ★ ★ ★

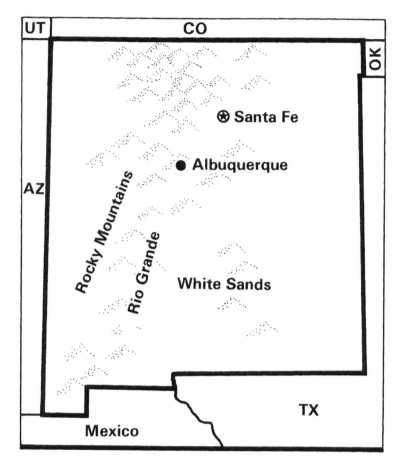

GEOFACTS

total area: 121,593 square miles
inland water: 258 square miles
population: 1,515,069
largest city: Albuquerque

GEOWORDS

moisture

Know New Mexico

1. Along New Mexico's northwest corner lies the land region called the _____ .

2. Rivers to the west of the Continental Divide flow toward the _____ .

3. Rivers to the east of the Continental Divide flow toward the_____ .

4. Short prairie grasses and sand dunes are part of New Mexico's _____

   region.

Map Study

1. Use blue to add the Rio Grande River and Pecos River to the map. Label the Pecos River.
2. Color the Rocky Mountains brown.
3. Color the area of the Colorado Plateau yellow.
4. Use a dotted line to show where the Continental Divide passes through New Mexico.
5. Color the states that border New Mexico orange. Color the country that borders New Mexico red.

 Our United States Geography Workbook

GEOFACTS
total area: 266,807 square miles
inland water: 4,790 square miles
population: 16,986,510
largest city: Houston

GEOWORDS
escarpment

Know Texas

1. Texas is the only state that was once a _____ .

2. Texas is made up of _____ major land regions.

3. The land of Texas tilts from _____ to _____ .

4. Yearly rainfall can vary in Texas from _____ inches in the Trans-Pecos region to

   _____ inches along the coastal areas.

Map Study

1. Trace the Red River and the Rio Grande River in blue. Color the Gulf of Mexico blue.

2. Color the Coastal Plain region green.

3. Color the states that border Texas orange. Color the country that borders Texas red.

4. Add five lakes to Texas. Label each lake. What can you tell about Texas land just by looking where the lakes are found?

5. Color the mountain area of Texas brown. Label these mountains ranges. You should have at least two labeled.

The Emigrants of the 1800s

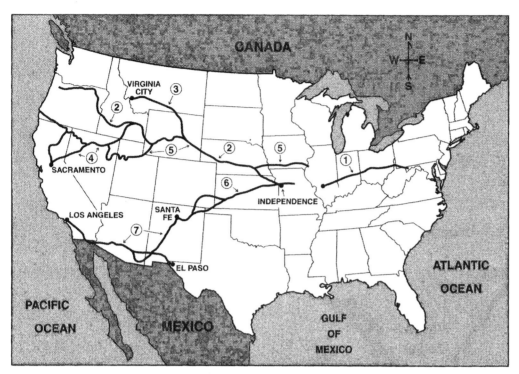

① THE NATIONAL ROAD   ③ THE BOZEMAN TRAIL   ⑤ THE MORMON TRAIL   ⑦ THE GILA TRAIL

② THE OREGON TRAIL   ④ THE CALIFORNIA TRAIL   ⑥ THE SANTA FE TRAIL

Maps and Measurement

Scale is used to show distance on a map. In using scale, a certain length of a line equals a certain number of miles on a map. For the emigrants map, use this scale:

1/4 inch = 115 miles

Now measure the length of the listed trails. Give the distance for each trail for as closely as you are able to measure it. (Be careful, some trails overlap.)

1. The National Road _____

2. The Oregon Trail from Independence to its end _____

3. The Bozeman Trail from Independence to Virginia City _____

4. The Santa Fe Trail from Independence to Santa Fe _____

5. The Gila Trail from El Paso to Los Angeles _____

 Our United States Geography Workbook

The Pacific Coast

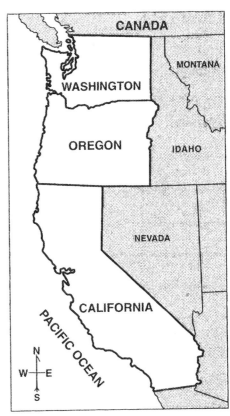

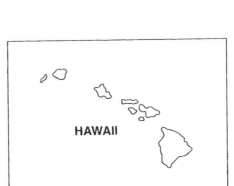

Map Study

1. Beginning in Idaho and Nevada, use red to add the Oregon Trail to the map. Use green to add the California Trail to the map.

2. Color the Pacific Ocean blue.

3. Use a star to show where each state capital is found. Label each city.

4. Draw arrows to show the direction of ocean currents along the coastlines of California, Oregon, and Washington.

The Pacific Coast

GeoThoughts

Think of what you have learned about the geography of the Great Plains and Rocky Mountain regions. Imagine yourself back in the 1840s, traveling along the Oregon Trail. Write a paragraph about one of your days of travel.

_____

_____

_____

_____

_____

_____

_____

_____

_____

_____

_____

 Spotlight

Thomas Bradley was the first African American elected mayor of Los Angeles. He was elected to five terms in office (1973-1989).

Thomas Bradley was born in 1917 on a cotton plantation in Calvert, Texas. He was the son of a sharecropper. He graduated from the University of California in 1940. Bradley served on the Los Angeles police department as well as on the city council.

Our United States Geography Workbook

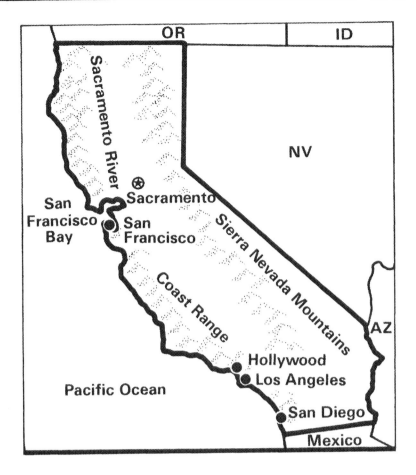

GEOFACTS
total area: 158,706 square miles
inland water: 2,407 square miles
population: 29,760,021
largest city: Los Angeles

GEOWORDS
fault line
aqueduct

Know California

1. California's greatest earthquake threat comes from the _____ fault.

2. Two deserts that cover the southeast corner of California are the _____ and the _____ .

4. _____ is used for bringing water to many of California's farm crops.

Map Study

1. Use blue to add the Sacramento River to the map. Then color the Pacific Ocean blue.
2. Color the Mojave Desert yellow. Color the Imperial Valley red. Label the desert and the valley.
3. Color the Sacramento Valley and the San Joaquin Valley tan. Label each valley.
4. Color the Sierra Nevada Mountains brown. Color California's coastal mountains orange.
5. Color the states that border California purple.

HAWAII ★

GEOFACTS

total area: 6,470 square miles
inland water: 45 square miles
population: 1,108,229
largest city: Honolulu

GEOWORDS

lava
reef

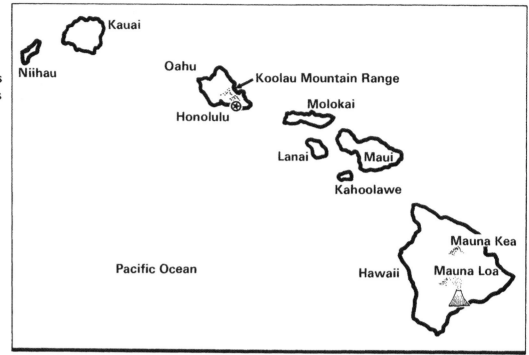

Know Hawaii

1. Hawaii is made up of _____ islands that stretch _____ miles.

2. Hawaii's _____ are built from grains of volcanic rock.

3. Hawaii's mountain area can get up to _____ of rain while the lowland areas may get only _____ of rain each year.

4. The first settlers in Hawaii came from the islands of _____ .

Map Study

1. Color the Pacific Ocean blue.
2. Find out what farm crops are grown on Hawaii's islands. Use symbols to show two farm crops for each island.
3. Use brown to show where Hawaii's mountain ranges are found.
4. Use a square to show where Hawaii Volcanoes National Park is found. Label the park.
5. Use yellow to color where dry areas are found in Hawaii.

 Our United States Geography Workbook

OREGON

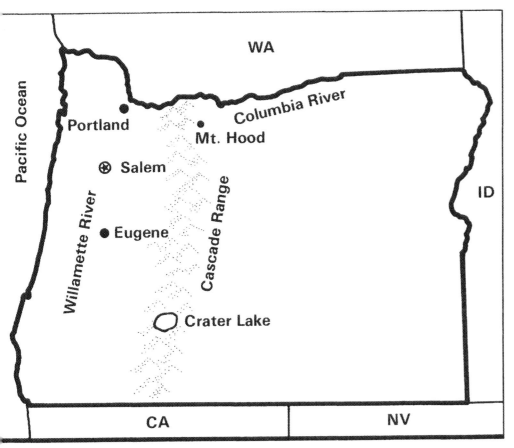

GEOFACTS
total area: 97,073 square miles
inland water: 889 square miles
population: 2,842,321
largest city: Portland

GEOWORDS
logjam

Know Oregon

1. Oregon is a leading state in _____ .

2. The _____ divide the land regions of Oregon.

3. The sale of flounder, salmon, tuna, and other _____ are important to the economy of Oregon.

4. Most of Oregon's 6,000 lakes are found among the _____ that cut across the state.

Map Study

1. Trace the Columbia and Willamette Rivers in blue. Use blue to add the Snake River to the map. Label the river.
2. Color the Pacific Ocean blue.
3. Color the Cascade Mountains brown. Add the Blue Mountains to the map. Label them and color them brown.
4. Color the Oregon coastline green.
5. Find out where Hell's Canyon is found. Label this place on the map.

WASHINGTON

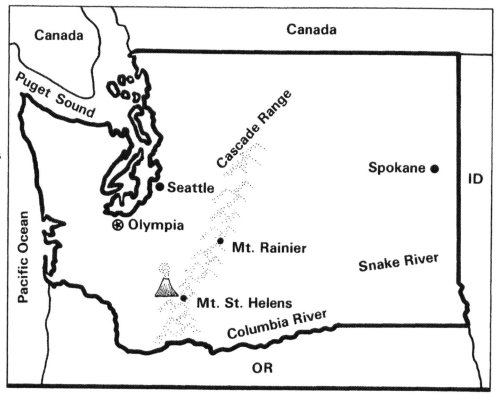

GEOFACTS
total area: 68,138 square miles
inland water: 1,627 square miles
population: 4,866,692
largest city: Seattle

GEOWORDS
pressure

Know Washington

1. Many of the mountains in the Cascade Range have thick layers of ice called _____ .

2. Northeast of the Cascade Mountains are the Rocky Mountains, also called the _____

    _____ .

3. Among Washington's Olympic Mountains are found lush _____ .

4. Fishing, logging, _____ and _____ products add to the

    economy of Washington.

Map Study

1. Use blue to trace the Columbia and Snake Rivers. Then color the Pacific Ocean and Puget Sound blue.
2. Color the Cascade Range brown. Using your mountain symbol and the color brown, add in the Rocky Mountains. Label the mountains.
3. Color the Columbia Plateau yellow.
4. Color the area of the Olympic Mountains green. Label the area.
5. Color the states that border Washington orange. Color the country that borders Washington red.

 Our United States Geography Workbook

★★U.S. Territories and Possessions

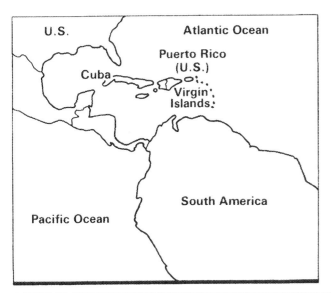

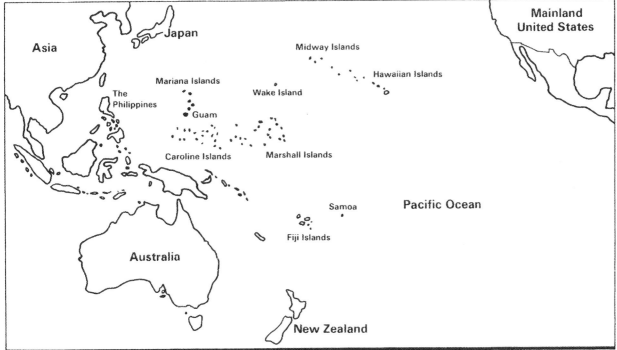

Map Study

1. Color the oceans in each map blue.

2. Draw a compass symbol on each map.

3. On the Atlantic Islands map, color Mexico orange, Central America green, and South America yellow.

4. On the Pacific Islands map, color the continent of Asia orange. Color the continent of Australia yellow.

Our United States Geography Workbook

U.S. Territories and Possessions

Make a Graph!

Use the information about the total land area of each territory and possession. Make a bar graph. Each bar s[...] be 1/2 inch wide. The bars should be 1/2 inch apart. Label each bar.

Color each bar a different color. Give the graph a title. The territories and possessions include Puerto Ric[...] Virgin Islands, Guam, Samoa, the Midway Islands and Micronesia.

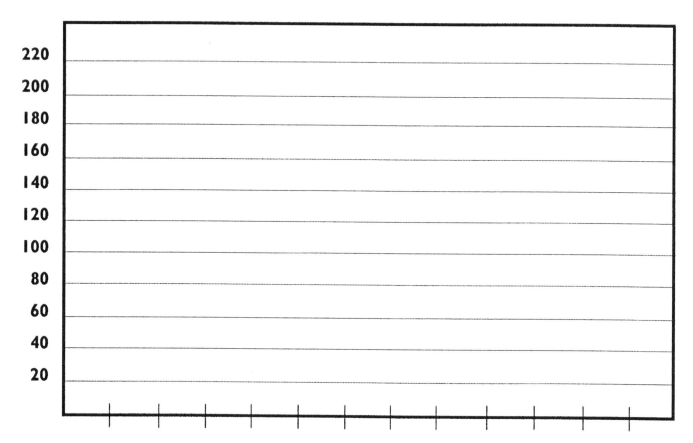

1. Which island group has the greatest amount of land area? _____

2. Which island group has the smallest amount of land area? _____

 Spotlight

Luis Muños Marín was Puerto Rico's first governor elected by the people (1948). Marín believed that Puerto Rico should be a commonwealth of the United States. Puerto Rico became a commonwealth of the United States on July 25, 1952.

Our United States Geography Workbook

GEOWORDS
typhoons

Know Puerto Rico

1. Puerto Rico is made up of several small _____ and one large island.

2. Puerto Rico gets most of its imports from the _____.

3. _____ is the main language of Puerto Rico.

Know the Virgin Islands

4. _____ main islands and _____ small islands make up the Virgin Islands.

5. The Virgin Islands began as _____ .

6. Three languages that are spoken in the Virgin Islands are _____ _____ .

Know the Pacific Islands

7. Guam has a coastline that is _____ miles long.

8. Guam has year round temperatures of between _____ and _____ degrees Fahrenheit.

9. Samoa is made up of _____ small islands.

10. Most of Samoa is covered by thick tropical _____ .

11. The Midway Islands are watched over by the _____ .

12. Wake, Wilkes, and Peale islands are watched over by the _____ .

13. Micronesia is made up of the island groups of _____ , _____ , and the _____ .

14. Altogether, _____ islands make up the Midway Islands.

15. The Midway Islands are protected by the _____ .